To David.

With Warmost Best Wishes
& thanks for all your help.

Ron.

BYD RON

●

RON'S WORLD

Heriaist, gorchfygaist heb gŵyn
Dreialon cadair olwyn;
Llenwaist ein bron â lluniau
Gymry'r oes â'th gamerâu.
Mae gweld gwlad drwy lygad lens
A'i selio, i ti'n sialens:

Rhoist enaid i'r tamaid tun
A'i harddwch i hen furddun,
A chawd rhwng dail "Llun a Chân"
Dy einioes di dy hunan.
Wyt yn gordial i'r galon
Na cheir ei well. Diolch, Ron.

Emyr Oernant

BYD RON · RON'S WORLD

RON DAVIES FDPS, ARPS, CPAGB, LMPA

CASGLIAD O FFOTOGRAFFAU 1944-2001

A COLLECTION OF PHOTOGRAPHS 1944-2001

LLYFRGELL GENEDLAETHOL CYMRU

THE NATIONAL LIBRARY OF WALES

2001

Argraffiad cyntaf – 2001

First Impression – 2001

ISBN 1 86225 032 4

Dyluniwyd ac argraffwyd gan Wasg Gomer, Llandysul.

Designed and printed by Gomer Press, Llandysul.

Cyflwynedig i'm teulu
a'm ffrindiau a phawb
am eu cymorth parod
ar hyd y blynyddoedd.

Ron.

This book is dedicated to
my family and friends
and all who helped me
over the years.

Ron.

DIOLCH I'R CANLYNOL AM EU CYFRANIADAU: MY THANKS TO THE FOLLOWING FOR THEIR CONTRIBUTIONS:

Alistair Crawford
Simon Evans
Mike Francis
W. J. Gruffydd
Dic Jones
Emyr Jones
Huw Ceiriog Jones
T. R. Jones
Vernon Jones
Eluned Phillips
J. R. Rees
Carwyn Rogers
Nicole Seebold
Nick Taylor
Llyfrgell Genedlaethol Cymru
Gwasg Gomer
Tŷ Nant Spring Water Limited

Tŷ Nant has a long established relationship with photographer Ron Davies, the company website acting as host for his work has been enhanced by the clarity and beauty of his images.

Tŷ Nant ~ *Images of Wales*, a calendar produced in association with the Wales Tourist Board, incorporated vivid pictures of daily life in Wales as well as the panoramic drama of his scenic photographs.

Rons' approach to life is visible throughout his work, his black and white images possess a clarity of vision, reflecting the land in which he was born and within which he plays so much a part. His abstract colour works represent his strength of character and determination to define himself through his works.

Nick Taylor, General Manager, Tŷ Nant Spring Water Ltd

SORRY, SIR, BUT YOU CAN'T GO THERE

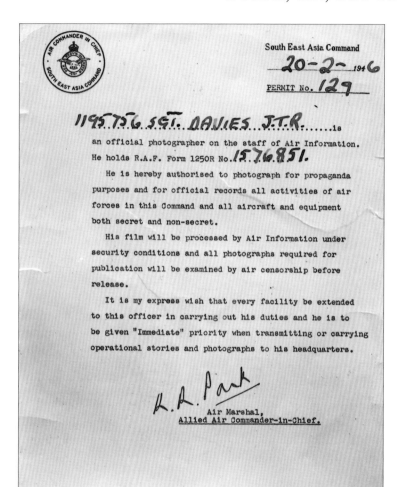

It was a long way from being a errand boy for Mr Evan John Thomas, MPS, chemist, in Aberaeron, West Wales, to becoming a war photographer: Ron Davies left school at sixteen, enlisted at eighteen in the Royal Air Force Voluntary Reserve, then, via a six month training programme as an instrument maker in 1940, he was sent to war at nineteen. There was, however, a connection from errand boy to war photographer for Mr Thomas also ran a developing and printing outlet, boasting D&P in only four hours, in order to beat his rival up the street who apparently could only boast seven. Thus an eight year old boy, who did not know what day of the week it was, except that he got 2 shillings a week for it, migrated to a darkroom and found magic, enough to last a life time, all because of an amateur photographer's enthusiasm; boys are always on the look out for a grown up secret to imitate. That magic in the developing dish was never to leave him, even now, and him looking forward to his 80th birthday on 17 December 2001.

The boy migrated from instruments to a young man servicing aircraft and was propelled to India, firstly Bombay, then up state to Santa Cruz, then Madras and Bangalore. You can't get more exotic than that, especially if you grew up in Aberaeron. Then he found himself and his friend Bert Melly with a steady little earner; the taking and making of photographs to send to the girls and the many mams back home. A chance encounter with a lift by the roadside, the Managing Director of Ilford in India, gave him a steady stream of silver coated paper and developing chemicals when a war was going on around him. Somebody must have noticed what he was up to, noticed the enthusiasm. No doubt they thought it would be cheaper to let him do it for real instead. So soon after the end of hostilities in 1946, he was made a war photographer and given a magic piece of paper, a passport to go where angels fear to tread and sent to Singapore, to Mountbatten's Headquarters, from whence he could cavort about in Sumatra, Java and Bali until his demob day in 1947. Then the dream came to a sudden end.

Back home in Aberaeron, the glamour days over, he faced a job as a painter and decorator with his father but even up the ladder with a paint brush in his hand he still had his camera. The war years changed so many lives. It has to be said for many that survived, for the better. The experience actually helped, especially such working class lads to engage with a world instead of a village, gave them the greatest education anyone could ever ask for, made them of independent mind. They now had a choice for the first time and were no longer necessarily going to do what was expected of them back home. Well, our boy was also unhinged and decided to make his move: to be like Evan Thomas who had first shown him those magic tricks in the dark. If he could clamber all over India and Indonesia he could travel round his Welsh hills, he could feel the wind once more in his hair, seek some excitement, push a boundary or two. By now he had enough experience of the portrait in the Sunday suit, the baby tucked in the shawl, the disorderly group that will not stand still outside the church door. Surely there was going to be at least as much money in this caper as in painting window frames while wishing you could just photograph the reflections instead.

Ron Davies is well known amongst his kith and kin as the local photographer, a man of all occasions, and all weathers, but he also became Ron Davies, well known Welsh landscape photographer, also the photographer of a passing world, especially of miners, of farm yard and farm field and now the passing of even the farmer. Yet his photography is always a celebration, of the extraordinary in the ordinary, a very Welsh love affair with his ain folk. He can even photograph images that can only be understood in the Welsh language, pictorial representations which he finds along the road side. For those in the know there is also a Ron Davies, press and television reportage photographer, years of it. He worked for *The Western Mail*, *Barn*, *The Express*, for the Welsh American newspaper *Y Drych*, for television, *BBC*, *TWW* then *HTV*. It was *Y Cymro* who gave him his first break in 1953, gave him a retainer that ended the benefit money and catapulted him into another world but one he was already familiar with, unknown to them, courtesy of the South East Asia Command. There he had rubbed shoulders with some of the big boys, journalists and photographers, who worked for the national press, like the *Daily Mirror, Daily Express, The Telegraph*. That training now paid off. Unknown, and more often than not without a credit, he became the photographer of down the pit, up the crane, of up and out by six a.m., of hours of waiting in the cold, the rain, of nothing caught today then, might as well go home; of the waiting for the phone call to tell him whether he was going to work the next day or not, just like those men waiting outside the factory gates hoping their faces would fit. Ron would say I exaggerate, he would say I had to do just whatever was needed to get the story as without it there would be no phone call to get the next one.

Encouraged by a growing appreciation in society, however, that photography could also be an art, material culture they now call it, as geographers via with art historians over what the likes of Ron Davies do everyday, now meant that photography could be a lot more than the newspaper story with the badly printed, cropped picture, all screwed up and chucked out with the left over fish and chips. In the wake of all the recent growth of cultural awareness came

photographic *distinction*; of Ron Davies' exhibitions, photographs with signatures, frames on gallery walls, in Wales and London and the USA, and who would have thought it, for just a photograph. There was to be photo shows with music and signed books of nothing but photographs, and who would have thought of that. Suddenly new generations began to knock on his door to ask the two bit local snapper what it was all about and the neighbours can't get their heads around any of that. And yes he did meet war photographer Cecil Beaton in Bombay all those years ago. And yes, I bet it surprises you that the local snapper knows all about the photographers you college boys are talking about now.

In 1984 I wrote of his book *Llun a chân*, 'The value in Ron Davies's photography is that we can be brought together, to feel for one another, to communicate. Look through the book, then look again, for he touches you, softly, quietly, at times almost apologetically.'

From distinction came the requests to teach, even now, he is still enjoying taking the beginners black and white class at the age of 79; beginners, advanced, colour, reportage, tell it to the amateurs, the degree students, even to their staff, tell it just wherever and whenever there is an opportunity to *enthuse*, tell everyone about all that black magic. It is as if there could be no end to catching everything that comes in front of the lens, and is not life wondrous and miraculous when seen through a view finder? Suddenly photography was no longer a solitary man out in the sun walking his solitary camera. Retirement has yet to happen to Ron, although he does not think he goes to work anymore, he just says he goes to make fun. Yet think of it, if he had the money, think what wonderful pictures he could make. So the struggle is never quite over, more's the pity, for many pay lip service to their culture, even adore cultural heroes, but few will part with a buck to help the effort of it all. Ron Davies is still at it, and we have to marvel at where it all comes from: 'What do you mean, Alistair, how old do I think I am? I never think of it. It's a good question. It is other people that are old, isn't it? I am not old in my head. You are only old when you catch yourself in the mirror. Takes you a bit by surprise then, doesn't it?'

Well, you could say that has to be the end of my story, that a photographer of some note can just as easily be found in a small sea-side town even if the media in capital cities don't seem to think so. But it is not, it is just the beginning of the tale. Not that Ron Davies would want me to tell you anymore of it, just as he conveniently forgot to tell the television company when he set out to be a roving news photographer with his secondhand 16 mm Bolex camera, only to end up arguing with a policeman to let him on to the site to do the needful, on to the ledge of the bridge over the river at Machynlleth in the dead of night while the divers were looking for the gun that shot the face off P.C. Rowlands. 'I'm sorry, sir, but *you* cant go there,' but it did not stop him. It did not stop him going down the pit with fellow Aberaeron artist George Chapman, or go up the crane. 'Excuse me, could you help me off of this wall. It's not a joke. It does not matter how I got on to the parapet. I just wanted to take photographs of the Houses of Parliament over there and this guy helped me up but then he left. I am not joking!! I can't get down. Please, can you get me off this bloody wall and back into my car?'

On 15 September 1950, one week after the new darkroom had been completed for the new exciting venture of 'Ron Davies, Aberaeron Photographer', he filled in as the not-much-good drummer for the band playing at the Air Wings Appeal dance at the Pier, Aberystwyth. At about 12 a.m. he left to go to Lampeter to photograph, in all their regalia, the Lampeter Show Committee at their annual ball. At 12. 30 a.m., on a bend on the B4337 Llanrhystud Road at Talsarn, travelling at no more than 10 miles per hour in second gear in his motorcycle and side car, the broken clip that held the canopy of the side car which he had noticed that morning and thought he must repair it soon, decided to let go. The canopy flew up and knocked him and the bike to the ground. His spinal cord snapped between vertebrae T4 and T5. Ron Davies became paralysed from the waist down and has spent the rest of his life in a wheelchair.

The day before, sitting on a bench, having a natter with a chum, saxophone player Jim Hayes, on the safety aspects of motorcycles and in particular the three wheeler, they concluded that it was extremely safe except for the tendency of the third wheel to lift up when going round a bend. After two years in the paraplegic unit at Southport Hospital, where naturally he became the unofficial resident photographer, complete with darkroom, after he had gone on strike and refused to carry on with his crochet and embroidery cushion covers, he returned home to another year of illness but he cut the benches in the darkroom down so that the enlarger could accommodate a wheelchair and decided to start *exactly* where he had left off. The very observant, and fellow photographers who see the world as a series of rectangles taken from fixed viewpoints, will have noticed that the majority of these photographs appear to have been taken either from the position of someone's groin or that the instigator must be a tiny person. Many are taken out of a car window even when they depict cows in a field by a river bank; if you want the picture you just drive the big Volvo to where the camera needs to be.

I once asked Ron what it felt like to have your life suddenly destroyed, your hopes and your dreams, what it felt like to have the rage of knowing your own mistake, or that the Fates one day had arbitrarily decided to cut your wings off. While Ron's pain is unique to him so too is his personality, he replied, 'But I was lucky, I still had my arms, you see, so I could still do what I wanted. With my arms I could still take photographs. It could have been a lot worse, couldn't it? I could have been blind. I could have died'.

I often wonder what gives him his courage. Is it just his personality, a genetic disposition? Or is it coupled to his unshakeable delight in making photographs. Could it be, could it just be, something that happened when he was about eight and saw the magic of the world come into focus in that dish of liquid, could it have burned so deep? Where does his spirit come from? It is a kind of blessing, given to us by him, totally unknown to him, of course, for he does not think of himself as either a hero or a shaman. This makes it sacred for he has no idea that coming off his bike 51 years ago, and all his subsequent labour and suffering; he has broken another 6 bones since the accident, actually grants to those who meet him something quite special. It confronts us with life: the fragility of it, the taking away of it, the ending of it, but also the *glory* of it. May he forgive me for telling you this part of his tale, especially if I tell you that it sometimes frightens me, frightens me that I may be unworthy of the feeling of it.

ALISTAIR CRAWFORD

Sarah Lambert, Aberaeron.

Paratoi am y Nadolig.

Preparing for Christmas.

Teyrnged i'r Meistr

Ers cyhyd ag y gallaf gofio, rwyf wedi mwynhau mas draw gwmnïaeth math arbennig o bobl. Sôn rwyf i, am y rhai sydd yn rhinwedd eu natur, a'u dull o gyflawni eu campau, yn gwneud i mi deimlo'n ostyngedig – nodwedd go brin ynof i! Hyd yma, nid oes llawer wedi gwneud hyn, ond rwy'n falch o gyfaddef fod Ron Davies yn un ohonynt.

Dros y blynyddoedd, cafwyd sawl cyhoeddiad ac arddangosfa o waith Ron, ac rwy'n siŵr y cawn lawer mwy eto. Fodd bynnag, mae *Byd Ron – Ron's World* yn gyhoeddiad arbennig iawn, ac yn garreg filltir bwysig yn hanes Ron. Bu'r dasg o olygu a dethol y lluniau yma yn un o'r tasgau golygu mwyaf dyrys a heriol a wynebwyd erioed gan artist byw 'wedwn i. Mae stiwdio Ron yn Aberaeron yn drysorfa o filoedd o luniau, bach a mawr, du a gwyn ac mewn lliw, yn adlewyrchu ystod eang o ddiddordebau personol, ac yn ymestyn dros flynyddoedd lawer o ymroddiad creadigol. Bydd ei ddetholiad terfynol o luniau yn sicr o gael ei ystyried yn un o'r casgliadau clasurol Cymreig mwyaf. Mae'n adrodd stori ryfeddol sy' tu hwnt i freuddwydion y mwyafrif ohonom. Mae'n fwy rhyfeddol fyth pan ystyriwn fod Ron y llynedd wedi dathlu 50 blwyddyn mewn cadair olwyn! (geiriau Ron, nid fy rhai i).

Pan ystyriwn bersonoliaeth Ron, ei chwilfrydedd naturiol, a'i gefndir mewn newyddiaduraeth, ynghyd â dogn helaeth o ddireidi a siniciaeth wleidyddol, nid yw'n syndod mai pobl a llefydd yw ei brif ysbrydoliaeth. Ychwanegwch ei ysbryd mentrus, a dyna i chi gymysgedd deniadol a thrawiadol o nodweddion.

Petaem yn disgrifio Ron Davies yn syml fel ffotograffydd Cymreig, byddem yn gwneud cam â'i ddawn ddiamheol fel athro deallus, a'i esiampl wych, di-lol i eraill sy'n dioddef o anabledd difrifol. 'F'anallu i symud yn rhwydd o le i le yw'r broblem, nid fy ngallu,' meddai Ron mewn cynhadledd genedlaethol ar Gyfle Cyfartal yn y Celfyddydau – cynhadledd y gwahoddwyd ef iddi fel cynrychiolydd gorllewin a chanolbarth Cymru. Dywedodd Ron y cyfan mewn deg eiliad, er i gynrychiolwyr eraill draethu'n faith. Ef a sbardunodd y syniad o ddarparu ystafell dywyll symudol 'Gofal Celf' – y gyntaf o'i bath, a alluogodd cannoedd o blant ac oedolion i brofi ffotograffiaeth mewn ardaloedd lle nad oedd dim cyfleusterau.

Rydym yn byw yn oes y camerâu di-ffwdan a di-ymdrech, sy'n ein harwain i gredu bod ffotograffiaeth da yn fater o bwyntio'r camera a chlicio'r botwm. Fodd bynnag, mae gwaith Ron Davies yn ein hatgoffa ni y gall ffotograffiaeth fod yn beth amgenach o lawer, ac mai'r hyn sy'n bwysig yw'r person y tu ôl i'r camera.

Yn fy marn i, nid Ron Davies yw testun y llyfr hwn, ond yn hytrach 'byd Ron Davies' – byd sy'n adlewyrchiad o'r bobl mae Ron wedi eu hadnabod, y llefydd yr ymwelodd â nhw, a'r Gymru mae'n garu a lle treuliodd y rhan fwyaf o'i oes.

Diolch i ti Ron am y fraint o gael gweld trwy dy lygad di.

Carwyn Matera Rogers,
Hydref 2001

A TRIBUTE TO THE MASTER

Ever since I can remember I have thoroughly enjoyed being in the company of those who by simply being who they are and doing what they do in the way they do it, reduce me to a state of uncharacteristic humility. To date there are very few who have succeeded in achieving this but I am proud to admit that Ron Davies ranks among the highest on the list.

There have been numerous publications and exhibitions of Ron's work over the years and I am in no doubt there are many more to come. *Byd Ron – Ron's World* however is a very special publication as not only does it mark a major milestone in Ron's life, it must have been one of the most difficult and challenging selection and editing exercises ever undertaken by a living artist. Ron Davies' studio in Aberaeron is literally littered with thousands of photographic images, large and small, colour and monochrome, covering a wide range of personal interest and spanning years and years of creative toil and artistic dedication.

His final selection of images will undoubtedly become one of the great collections of photographic images to be linked to Wales, as it tells a remarkable story and takes us on a journey which most of us can only dream of. Even more remarkable when we take into account of the fact that last year Ron Davies "celebrated his 50th year in a wheelchair", his words not mine!

With his natural inquisitiveness and journalistic roots it is not surprising that people and places are Ron's major source of inspiration – add an undercurrent of wicked humour and a healthy dose of political cynicism and an always present sense of artistic adventure and you end up with a punchy and seductive artistic cocktail.

To describe Ron Davies simply as a Welsh photographer would be to deny him his rightful place as a talented and clever teacher, and as a robust and no nonsense role model for others like him who suffer from severe physical disabilities.

'Mobility is my problem not ability', said Ron in a national conference on Equal Opportunities in the Arts to which he had been invited as the delegate for mid and west Wales. Other delegates spoke for much longer periods. Ron said it all in less than ten seconds. It was he who spearheaded ARTS Care/Gofal Celt's mobile disabled darkroom – the first of its kind and which has enabled hundreds of children and adults to taste and savour the experience of photography in areas where facilities simply did not exist.

We live in times when pointing and clicking our throw away idiot proof cameras makes for good photography or so we are led to believe. However Ron Davies' work serves as a salutary reminder that there is much more to photography then that, and that it is *who* is behind the camera that counts.

In my view the subject of this publication is not Ron Davies, rather it is the 'world of Ron Davies' – a world dominated by the people he has met, the places he has visited and the Wales which he has loved and lived in for most of his life.

Thank you Ron, for lending us your eyes.

CARWYN MATERA ROGERS,
October 2001

Bombay.

Srinigar, Kashmir.

Llyn Dâl, Srinigar, Kashmir.

Dâl Lake, Srinigar, Kashmir.

Srinigar, Kashmir.

Srinigar, Kashmir.

4

Cwch Preswyl, Llyn Dâl, Srinigar, Kashmir.
House Boat, Dâl Lake, Srinigar, Kashmir.

Llyn Dâl, Srinigar, Kashmir.   Dâl Lake, Srinigar, Kashmir.

Tacsi Dŵr, Srinigar, Kashmir.   Water Taxi, Srinigar, Kashmir.

6

Bangalore, India.

Pwll Glo Wattstown, De Cymru - tudalennau 8 i 16.   Wattstown Colliery, South Wales – pages 8 to 16.

Sbragwr a'i gyfeillion.

A Sprager (brakeman)
and his mates.

Mynd i lawr.   Going Down.

Diwedd y sift.

End of shift.

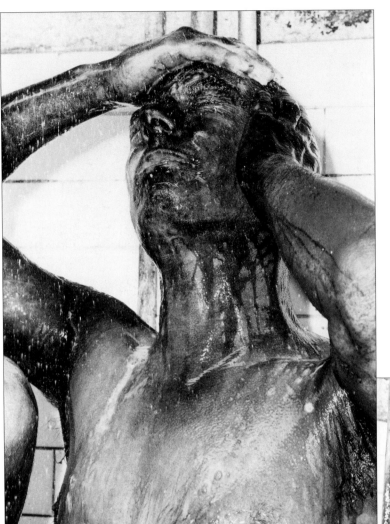

Baddon y lofa.

Pithead Baths.

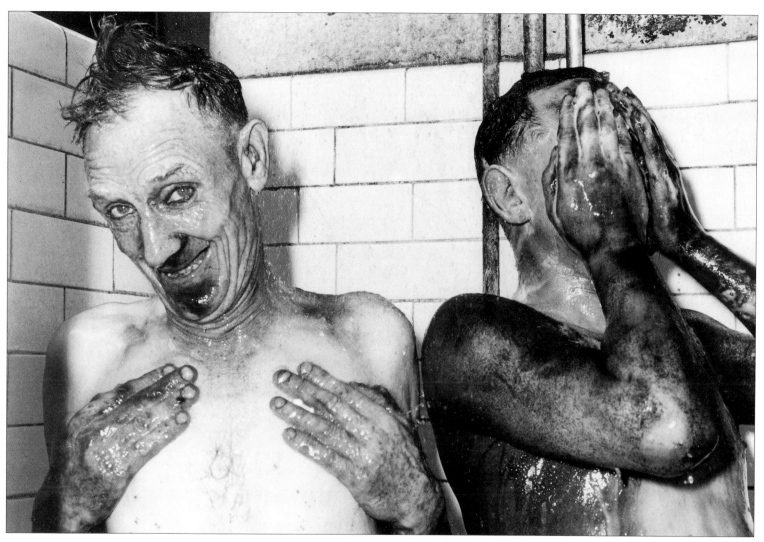

'Don't take me now, I'm shy see.'

Bois y banc.

Surface workers nick-named 'The Sunshine Boys'.

Prentisiaid.

Apprentices.

Michael Evans a Francis John, Aberaeron.

Michael Evans and Francis John, Aberaeron.

Rhieni Maeth   Foster Parents.

Techneg dyn greodd Doli – yr un dawn
a fedrai greu Dandi
y ceffyl sy'n synnu ni,
a'i chwerthin yn ein sobri.

Os yw'r duwiau brwdfrydig a'u pyls ar
greu campweithiau lloerig,
pa fwystfil o waed a chig
ddaw nesaf o'u dychymig?

     *   *   *

Tractor mewn clawdd heb injin, fu'n foddion
i'r ceffyl 'ma chwerthin.
Gweld ei hun eto'n frenin
wedi'r holl flynyddoedd blin.

        Eluned Phillips

Dic Jones, Yr Hendre, Blaenannerch, Ceredigion.

David James, Llangeitho a Will Morgan, ffarmwr o Dalsarn, Ceredigion.

David James, Llangeitho and Will Morgan, farmer, Talsarn, Ceredigion.

John Price, gof Talsarn, Ceredigion a'i ferch Gwyneth a'i fab David yn rhwymo olwyn cart.

John Price, blacksmith, Talsarn, Ceredigion with his daughter Gwyneth and son David, bonding a cartwheel.

Mari'r Felin (Mary Evans),
Pontrhydfendigaid.

Wil Jones a Fred Llewelyn ar lan afon Teifi, Cenarth.   Wil Jones and Fred Llewelyn on the banks of the river Teifi, Cenarth.

Ivor, Trefor a Dan, y brodyr Jenkins, pysgotwyr, Aberaeron. Ivor, Trefor and Dan, the Jenkins brothers, fishermen, Aberaeron.

Phill Davies a gwerthwr winwns o Lydaw,
'Shoni Winwns', Aberaeron.

Phill Davies and a Breton onion seller,
'Shoni Winwns', Aberaeron.

Ffair Feigan, Crymych.

Hippy Festival, Crymych.

Stella Jones, Aberaeron.

Meinwen am fod yn fenyw;
Dan yr het mae dawn ei rhyw.

T. Llew Jones

Heol Pontarfynach.   Devil's Bridge Road.

Golchi defaid, afon Teifi, Cenarth.

Washing sheep, river Teifi, Cenarth.

Nant-y-moch, yng ngolau'r lleuad.   Nant-y-moch, by moonlight.

Gosod clawdd, Gwent.

Hedging, Gwent

Cors Caron.

Tregaron Bog.

Un gusan felys yn y gwynt
Sy'n dala rhamant dyddiau gynt.

Vernon Jones

Pum poni Penbont ar Gors Goch Caron

Pum poni ar Gors Caron
uwch twf y misoedd tirion,
ar grwydr haf yn mynd a dod
cyn dyfod gaeaf creulon.

Mae llain o wyrddni ara'
lle nad yw'r brwyn yn dagfa;
deng mil blynyddoedd yn hen hoen
dan groen yr erwau yma.

Tu draw i'r llain mae'r gawnen
yn etifeddes lwydwen;
y tyfiant gwyllt sy piau tir
yr hytir lle mae'r fawnen.

Ond coed sy'n wyrdd ar lechwedd
a gorwel glas i'r tirwedd;
mae rhin Gorffennaf trwm ei glod
heb ddarfod, yma'n gorwedd.

Rhan o draddodiad Cardi
ar Gors Goch eto 'leni;
yn un o fintai'r cobiau hardd
a dardd yn Sir Aberteifi

John Roderick Rees

Five Penbont ponies on Cors Caron

On this green island
in the Red Bog,
five are corralled
behind the pale fog.

Penbont ponies
in a kind July
and the hazy sunshine
drifting by.

Two white blazes
busy on grass;
one in meditation
two with a secret to pass.

Deep in its frame
the Teifi glides
and the myth of Pont Einon
eternally hides.

Five Welsh cobs
of a timless brand,
their yesterdays rooted
in Cardi-land.

John Roderick Rees

35

However hard the climb, there is a way
To guide us to the pasture whence we stray.

Vernon Jones

Golygfa o Heol B4391, Bala i Ffestiniog.

View from B4391 Road, Bala to Ffestiniog.

Rhosgadfan, Eryri.

Rhosgadfan, Snowdonia.

John Price, Gof, Talsarn.   John Price, Blacksmith, Talsarn.

Dave Petersen, San Cler.

Dave Petersen, St. Clears.

Aber Glaslyn, Porthmadog.

Glaslyn Estury, Porthmadog.

Afon Menai.

Menai Straits.

Harbwr Aberaeron.

Aberaeron Harbour.

Machlud Haul, Aberdyfi.

Sunset, Dyfi Estuary.

Bwlch Abergwesyn.

Abergwesyn Pass.

Cors Fochno.

Borth Bog.

Cronfa Pen-y-garreg, Cwm Elan.

Pen-y-garreg dam, Cwm Elan.

Tal-y-llyn.

Fairbourne.

Machlud haul dros Fae Ceredigion.

Sunset over Cardigan Bay.

Aberystwyth.

Llyn Tegid.   Bala Lake.

Afon Tywi ar
ôl haf sych.

River Towy
after a dry
summer.

Llyn Brianne.

TANYGRISIAU

Esgyn y mwg o aelwyd y chwareli
Yn darth croesawgar dros y grisiau gwych,
Tra'r teiau sgwâr a gwres trydanol Stwlan
Trwy lygaid oer yn rhythu'n syber sych.

Vernon Jones

Llanberis. Hen Chwarel Lechi Dinorwig.

Llanberis. Old Dinorwic Slate Quarry.

Tal-y-llyn.

Y Mwmbwls, Abertawe.   Mumbles, Swansea.

Glofa'r Marine.

Marine Colliery.

Eglwys Y Mwnt, Ceredigion.

Mwnt Church, Ceredigion.

Tal-y-llyn.

Llanafan.

Trefdraeth. Newport.

Nantgwynant.

Ysbyty Bronglais Hospital, Aberystwyth

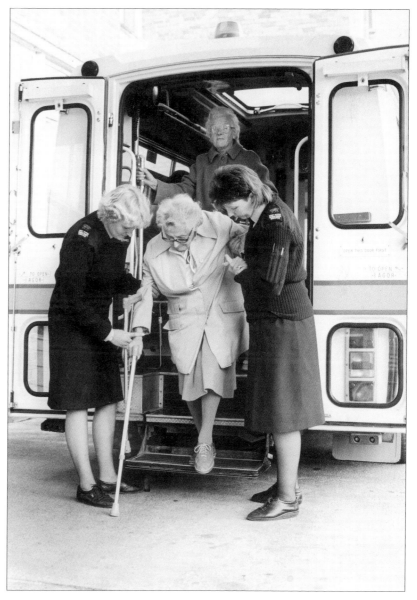

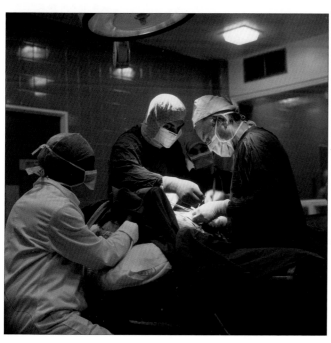

Bywyd gwyllt.

Wild life.

Pen-caer, Sir Benfro.   Strumble Head, Pembrokeshire.

Bannau Brycheiniog.   Brecon Beacons.

Pwll Glo'r Twr, Hirwaun.

Tower Colliery, Hirwaun.

Bwlch Abergwesyn.

Abergwesyn Pass.

Llyn Ogwen, Eryri.

Ogwen Lake, Snowdonia.

Llyn Mymbyr.

Mymbyr Lake.

Llyn Gwynant, Eryri.

Gwynant Lake, Snowdonia.

Llyn Tegid, Y Bala.

Llyn Fron Goch, Trisant, Ceredigion.

Eryri.   Snowdonia.

Eglwys Gadeiriol Tŷ Ddewi.

St. David's Cathedral.

To Eglwys Gadeiriol Tŷ Ddewi.

Roof of St. David's Cathedral.

Bettws Ifan, Ceredigion.

Aberaeron.

Harbwr Aberystwyth.   Aberystwyth Harbour.

Abergwaun.

Fishguard.

Winston Evans, Cei Newydd.

Winston Evans, New Quay.

Breuddwydion Melys. Harbwr Aberaeron.

Sweet Dreams. Aberaeron Harbour.

79

Fferm Bryn Amlwg, Penuwch, Ceredigion.   Bryn Amlwg Farm, Penuwch, Ceredigion.

Blaenau Ffestiniog.

Pentir Cei Newydd o Draeth y De, Aberaeron.   New Quay Head from South Beach, Aberaeron.

Cwm-yr-eglwys, ger Abergwaun.

Cwm-yr-eglwys, near Fishguard.

Llyn Brianne.

Cronfa Claerwen, Cwm Elan.

Claerwen Dam, Elan Valley.

Pentre Elan.

Elan Village.

Cefn-hir, Llyn Cregennen, Cader Idris.

Llyn Gwynant, Eryri.

Gwynant Lake, Snowdonia.

Cwm Rheidol.

Tal-y-llyn.

Cwm Rheidol.

Llanrhystud.

Ger y mynediad i Orsaf Drydan
Dinorwig, Llanberis.

Near the entrance to Dinorwic Power
Station.

Cwm Ystwyth.

Llanrhystud.

Cystadleuaeth Aredig, Llangoedmor, Ceredigion.   Welsh Ploughing Championship, Llangoedmor, Ceredigion.

Camu'n gyson o wrych i wrych
Un troed ar y grwn a'r llall yn y rhych,
Y mynd a'r dod yn agosau
A'r cefnau coch yn cywrain gau.

Vernon Jones

Ystumtuen, Ceredigion.

Ystumtuen, Ceredigion.

Chwarel Llechwedd.

Y Chwarelwr

Rhywiog yn wir yw'r maen ar bwys ei glun
Ac ynddo'n ddiau ddeunydd cerrig bras,
Cyson yw clec ei ordd ar ben y cŷn
Wrth hollti'r clwt yn dudalennau glas.
Dysgodd ei grefft yng ngholeg taid a thad,
Cyn dyfod ar y fasnach lechi drai,
Pan droes y töwyr at ddefnyddiau rhad
Aeth pris ei fargen yntau'n llai a llai.

Llechwedd Slate Mine.

Bellach dirywiodd ei hen grefft i fod
Yn arddangosfa i ymwelwyr haf,
Y miloedd heintus sydd yn mynd a dod
Dros ael y domen pan fo'r hin yn braf,
Ni welir yn y llun ei lofrudd cudd
Yn aros yn llechwraidd am ei ddydd.

T.R. Jones

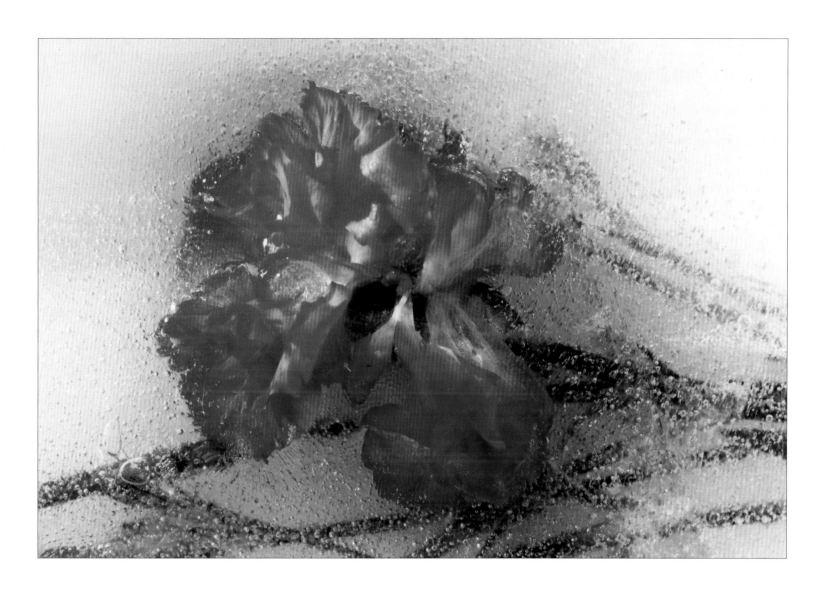

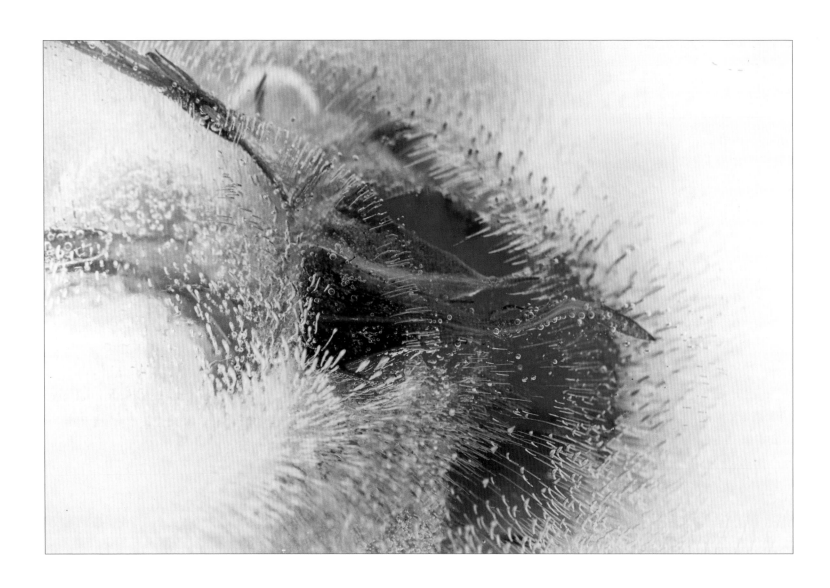

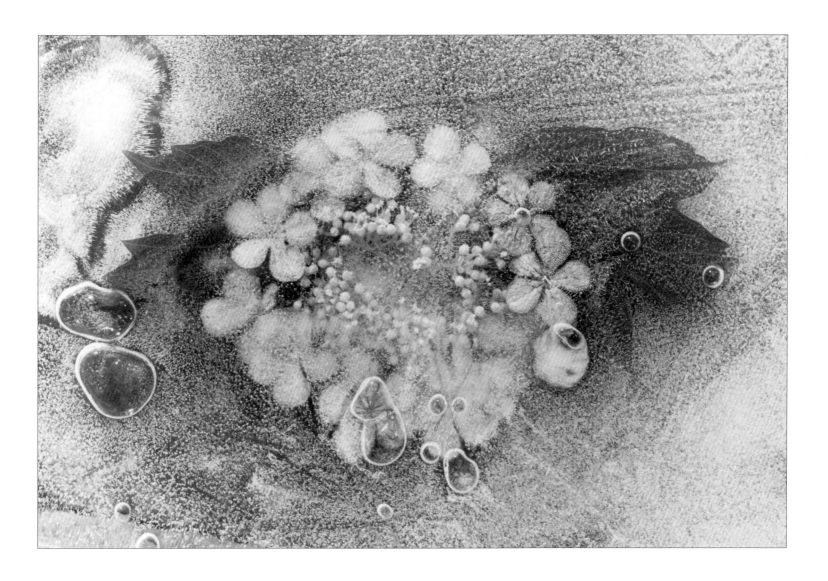

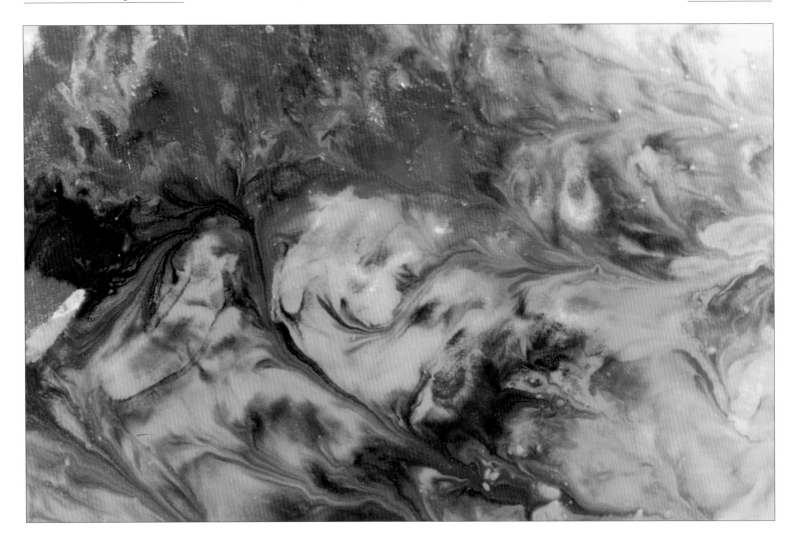

I'r ychydig unigryw – ordeiniwyd
Gorau dawn dynolryw
I wneud yr hyn nad ydyw
A'r hyn na fu'n rhan o fyw.

In our ravings for ever – are arrayed
The dream and the nightmare.
The witch and the elf are there
Fuelled in fancy's fire.

Dic Jones

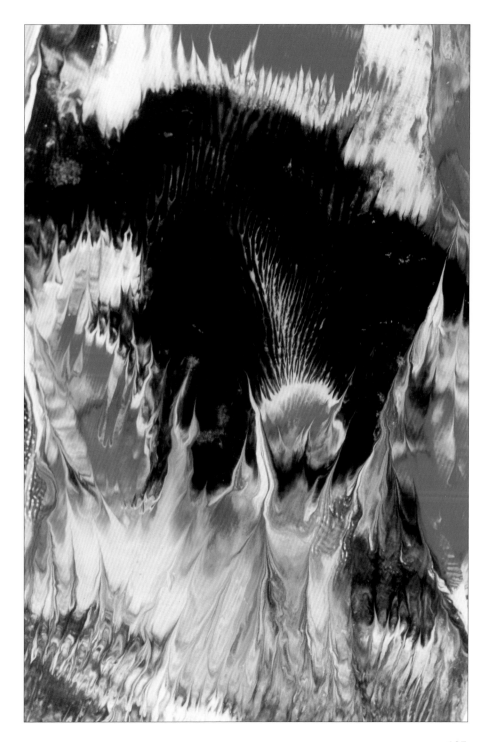

110

Ym mwynder Dyfed,
Yng Ngwlad Brynach a Dewi
Rhwng Carn Ingli a Phen Crugiau
Mewn hafn o wastadedd
Mae eglwys Nanhyfer a'i thŵr militaraidd
Yn bugeilio'r coed, a'r afon, a'r beddau . . .

W. J. Gruffydd

Yr Ywen Waedlyd, Nanhyfer.

The 'Bleeding' Yew tree, Nevern.

112

Cefn yr Ywen Waedlyd.

Back of 'Bleeding' Yew tree.

Yn y dechreuad yr oedd y Chwedl –
Ar gangen o'r ywen hon ym mynwent Nanhyfer
Crogwyd gŵr ifanc ar gam . . .
Mae'r gwaed yn diferu o hyd o dristwch y pren
A'r goeden felltigedig yn gwyro'n euog tua'r llawr.
Yn Nanhfyer heno –
Mae crawc stwrllyd y brain ar y brigau;
Sŵn yr afon yn dianc am ei bywyd i'r môr;
A'r ywen yn gwaedu ddydd a nos uwch gweddillion y beddau.

W. J. Gruffydd

Tair troedfedd ar ddeg o groes Geltaidd
Yn dal a gosgeiddig o dan haul a lleuad.
Ar y seithfed o Ebrill dôi'r gog i ganu ar ei phen.
Mae'r ysgrifen gyfrin ar ei bron
A'r cylch tragwyddol o gwmpas y groes.
Bu addolwyr defosiynol yn penlinio o'i blaen
Cyn dychwelyd am byth i'r pridd a'r llwch
Yn y gors a'r mynydd, ac o dan y garreg ogam.

W. J. Gruffydd

Hen yw'r meini megalithig
Sy'n gwylio bedd yr Hil.
O dan eu cadernid a'u cyfaredd
Mae helwyr beiddgar a'u gwragedd ffrwythlon
Yn cysgu yn y gromlech baganaidd yn y graig.

O'u cwsg hir
Deuant yn ôl i hela yn y fforest dragwyddol.

W. J. Gruffydd

Tanygrisiau.

Drws beudy – fferm Troedrhiwsebon, Cwm Rheidol, Ceredigion.

Cowshed door – Troedrhiwsebon farm, Cwm Rheidol, Ceredigion.

Talcen y beudy – fferm Troedrhiwsebon.

Gable-end of the cowshed – Troedrhiwsebon farm.

Aber y Ddyfi.

Dyfi Estuary, Aberdyfi.

Abereiddi, Sir Benfro.

Abereiddi, Pembrokeshire.

Ger Llanfarian, Ceredigion.

Near Llanfarian, Ceredigion.

Pumlumon.

Mynydd Preseli, Maenclochog.

Diwrnod o hwyl, Aberaeron.   Fun day at Aberaeron.

Steve Jones, Aberaeron.

Hippy.